I0161781

Anti Anxiety Relief
Easy Ways to Leverage Stress

**Unload Tension-
Avoid Panic**

Aka-Linseed Wright

Printed by- **Create Space.com**

Expressions of Gratitude

My humble thanks to the Sovereign Lord Jehovah, God- psalms 73:28. The one who gave me insight to use wisdom and depth to follow the natural, meditative course than panic anxiety, during spousal trauma, family and friends for their support to continue my writing passion, Akira Graphics for cover design, Create Space in editing layout and proofreading span; Fanstory.com for their help in shaping needed poetry skills.

The United States of America has typed stamped and published this book.

ISBN-13:978-0615981611
ISBN-10:0615981615

Aka-Linseed Wright
Connection: Whitehall P.A.
484-221-8053

Table of Contents

Chapter One

Exceptional Award Poetry Verse 2013

Fallen Shadow

Dreams, and goals rocket to the sky.
Guy feels strong sense of accomplished
Pride.
His gut reaction displays love, power fame
and acclaim.
All pulled from a winning victory game.
Bang! In walks unseen foil, catastrophic
scent for embarrassment. The embroiled
Passion road to lament.
Shots fired in the dark. It is tricky mind
intruder fantasy.
Scary. Yet it seemed to be reality.
Sorrow unfolds by fallen shadow in shear,
tragedy. anxiety.
Identity shock to his sanity.
"He didn't know," says Guy. A close friend dies,
in the wrong place.
Face now mourning, inside the cemetery gate,
Now, unsure of his grace.

Chapter Two

Judges Excellent Selections
2013 Poems

Boston Marathon-Joy and Grief

The eyes are on a special event
Runners all race to the end line.
Caught by a surprise explosion,
the real scene is chaos.
They run for cover.
Death took a young boy,
happy in
Boston
Why?

Aka-Linseed Wright

Mind Blowers Shanghai

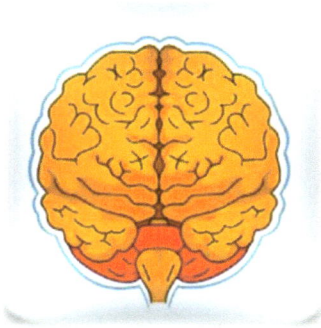

Hot summer embraced the world, in a roasting
Climate change.
Sustained temperature heat, scorched day after day.
Great drama scenes happened as the season 2013
wane away.
Multiple tasks left undone. The Sun remains.
Brain drain takes over once again!
Amidst rocky road bumps, cracked ruts and soggy
rain, plans that were sound got turned around in vain.
In reasonable explanation, they tried to be polite with
insight but deep down, hankering within, they vowed to
make gain from their wealthy, aged kin.
Trickiness lay hatched around the bin for Gin.
The unwary victim cringed in horror. It was an orchestrated
drama that caused increased trauma.
Felt like she had stepped, on slippery gravel in travel.
She sensed something wasn't right and needed
a speedy flight.
Amidst siblings who knew her plight, she couldn't sleep
soundly that night.
Nodding her head in cat nap, Gin plotted her sneak
counter attack.

Aka-Linseed Wright

Mind Blowers Shanghai

She had to escape from the mind blowers shanghai trap.
Her victory lawyer was on the map.
Next day, being shrewd, was her chance for freedom to try.
Scurrying across the road to the police, came sanctuary
and her glory for being alive.
Back home, legal charges would be imposed
Against some kin, who showed little love or motherly
compassion.
Now their faces are without a grin or inherited stipend.

Mischievous Weapon
   Unwise course

sly cutting ambush
little organ in the mouth
ambiguous blade

Autumn in Mirror Harvest
   Captivating prism colors

Winds whip
through the tree limbs
as leaves reveal bare bones.
Burnt orange leafs crackle on road
Fall's Song

Faith Wobble
   Unsteady gait

faith sometimes wind swept
choice hush range,
along jagged rocks

Aka-Linseed Wright

Memory Tribute to "The King of Pop"

Few people could top him in the
glamor and glitter shop.
His release of "Thriller" a chillier
Remains top.
No entertainer has matched his
flair or great choreographer,
In the chair.
He had the beat, walk and pizazz,
gifted talents displayed; shared.
In thinking, a little like Fred Astaire.
Mass fan mania, tears, screams;
fainting spells do tell!
Your mesmerizing personality is
what did sell.
A magnetic rocket excitement, all
could see attraction energy!
Moon walk action, you left behind
with great satisfaction.
Yet there were horrid, life momentous
days, as ruin grapes, on the vine to
Face.

Aka-Linseed Wright

Memory Tribute to "The King of Pop"

Oh worried man, unable to sleep.
Fears have many companions it keeps.
Who can know when death knocks?
Your life is over by its clock.
Central trauma closed. "The King of Pop"
His real life drama was not karma.

Winter Walks Around
Winter in person

His bellowing howl swirls in
with whipping tree limbs
as teapot on the stove squeals,
Winter walks around

Apartment Upstairs Chicanery
Senior age gap

Downstairs lady wears thorn face
Upstairs, stuff hits floor
Golden Age culture gauntlet

Aka-Linseed Wright

Black Crow Communicates
Noisy bird at daybreak

Black crow noise maker caw, caw, caw on limb
Baby fledgling flutters on ground
Mother crow fully yap, yaps
The male genus swoops down
Talons grab gently,
baby rescued
Flight test ends
Hush.

[Writer]
Mind in design

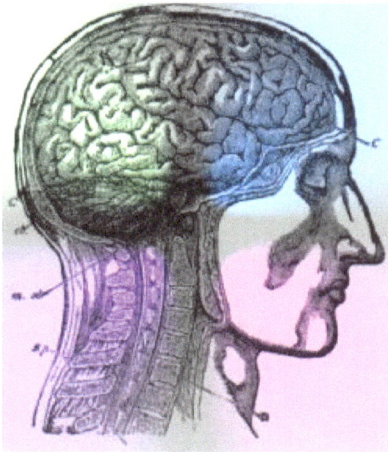

When ideas ascend
Round and round in
Isles of thought
To assemble court,
Even so my dear
Reflections are clear

Aka-Linseed Wright

Affirm
First letter spells word

Astute integrity choice
For
Favor
In Retrospect
Moral

Death Rattle
Mouth hazard

Psyche decision
inferior to his life.
Brags by active choice
reveals on a sadly act,
the path to shear collapse.

Impact
verdict closure

Inside the chamber room
Michael's silence spoke about
past reflections
associated with corrections for
Trial verdict closure

Failure Mask
Tribute to Steve Jobs

Failure in disguise is a
step-by-step tracks to success
that requires persistence

Aka-Linseed Wright

Her Warning Signs Ignored
Life addiction ruin

Her world of logic had changed
when drug dependency reigned.
The endangered one a seal she became.
Her world of logic had changed.

Warning signs friends recalled and ignored.
Too. See the swimming pool a notable clue!
Her world of logic had changed
when drug dependency reigned

Suspicion
Without all facts

Safeguard
Uneasiness
Stain
Proposal
Insight
Camouflaged
Insinuated
Orchestrated
Narrow mind

Rocksteady's Bachelorhood

Bachelor playing monkeyshines

Rhonda's face was discolored and distraught
In flashback mode she deeply thought.

Love had bloomed in the Red Rose Lagoon,
As she hummed, here comes the bride; groom.

Rocksteady said, "Say what?" Dear you're out
Of sorts, my bachelorhood will never be caught."

Her face recovered from the stain of emotional gloom.
Rhonda realized that love can be eroded doom!

Aka-Linseed Wright

Mouth Shock
Worker conflict

Shocking day, boss said, "You're fired!"
Something came across both his ears.
Big competitor conflict.
But, it was my day off.
There was no contract,
survival key.
Non employ
not for
me.

Keep Marriage Healthy
Work in unity

Godly loving yoke
Inbred need in attraction,
strong heartfelt feelings,
focus on the moral side
The best love nuptial union.

Aka-Linseed Wright

Snow vortex Lune
Below zero in PA

Snow returns water
while snow snaps
along east coast

Cherry Blossoms Echo Spring
Spring season

Bright pink glow fills the sky
is dazzling in spring light.
Solely the Cherry Blossoms
do not stay around.
How can that be?

Life in Metamorphosis
Coping with Challenges

Let the peace of God come into your life
during frustration.
Stop fighting the elements and let him in
for consolation.
When life takes a wrong turn as your behavior
turns to disdain.
It's definitely time to let his Holy Spirit shine,
from deep within.

Why don't you let him in?

Focus Eyes
Owl Vision

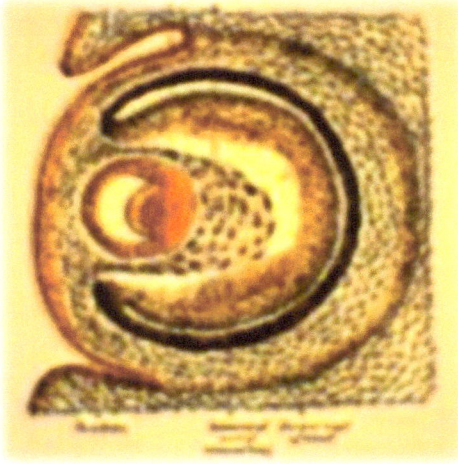

Fully unburden valueless distractions
Offset
Confusion
Usually
Senseless to great achievement

Eyes
Yield
Excellent
Service

Chapter Three

Fanstory Poetry Reviews
2012-2013

Fallen Shadow

I enjoyed the compact rhyme in this piece and the surprise it brought. The poem tries to retain the sense of tragedy, where others might seek blame. – Laurie

Boston Marathon – Joy And Grief

Awesome, but really sad. I feel extreme sympathy for the young boy, as well as, the people in Boston. I also mourn for the victims of this terrible tragedy – DRG2

Mind Blowers Shanghai

I liked the detail of setting and alliteration, in the rocky roads bump line. Good internal rhyme in sound in got turned around. Good alliteration in sleep soundly. An interesting story of intrigue reading. – adeiupearl

Mischievous Weapon

Perfect form. You did a perfect job describing the tongue. Being small the tongue can create huge catastrophes. Well done. – D.Steiner

Autumn In Mirror Harvest

You said it best with your poetry. It amazes me when you paint such a vivid picture with such few words. I liked the thought that went with it. – Kleck

Faith Wobble

Yes our walk in faith can be hard for Christians as we face trials, tribulations; non-believers. Our saving grace is God, who walks with us. Our Lord free of sin was not tempted by the evil one. – Sue

Memory Tribute to The "King of Pop"

I really liked this. It's hard to believe, it is 3 years already! Poem shows deep feeling and respect for a brilliant talent, who left us too soon. – Linda

Winter Walks Around
Easy to imagine this one. The teapot is a comfort against the winter's cold winds and icy trappings. You've certainly written of it well, in this great Nanni. – Gungalo

Apartment Chicanery
I admired your story in this tiny verse. Coincidentally, I recently heard a similar tale. I liked your minimal style. – John

Black Crow Communicates
Wonderful Nonet and a great little tale. You did a superb job of telling this one, and it even fits the regulations, the way it should. – Gungalo

[Writer]
So much wisdom penned in your offering. I know because at age 73, I am still evolving. Every time I see the picture of the Thinker, it reminds me of a previous tot, I do Nanny Care for. He is very precocious. Now 4 but I remember age 2. He was staring at something intently. His mother asked him, what was he doing? He said, "I am thinking!" – Jean

Affirm
A solid Acrostic for Affirm. Good touch of alliteration in favor, good consonance of R in retrospect moral. A thoughtful look at human behavior and ethics. – Brooke

Death Rattle
   You have executed the construction of a Tanka admirably. You move the reader with intensity of your words. – Saucy

Impact
   You did a good job on your poem and those past reflections bring to my mind. Take a good look at the man in the mirror…My verdict is you did a great job! – Songbird

Failure Mask
   Great Tribute to Steve Jobs. The poem kept the right syllable count and conveyed an upbeat, positive message. A very good job! – honeydo51

Her Warning Sign Ignored
   This is a fine tribute to Whitney…her voice was golden for sure, as you put it, crystal. Thank you…This touched. – Dinah
   Great tribute to a lovely lady. It is so sad that the world got to her. Such a voice…You have honored our lady with your fine words. –S.Asbury

Suspicion
   I loved this piece very much and the message. The presentation was awesome. I appreciate your notes. The words selected were direct and appropriate. This piece is worth every star. – Saucy

Rocksteady's Bachelorhood
   If marriage wasn't invented, women wouldn't suffer so much. Our abuse of love, not because we're doing it on purpose but for some of us, it takes to long to find out what is what? I liked it very much. – Ruskin

Rocksteady's Bachelorhood

Wow what an unexpected ending to this story, in a poem. Very well written piece, describing love and loss. Well done. – Steve

Mouth Shock

It was good and very clear. Mouth Shock. Losing your job put your ears to shock. Pleasure reading and well done. – donette

Keep Marriage Healthy

Very good poetic write, to focus on the moral side of marriage. The poem is symbolic of a true, "God-loving yoke." – dandanthnyt

Snow Vortex

Meantime in sunny New Zealand…This reminds me how strange it is that one of the driest places in your house is inside the refrigerator…I like the clever use of cold snaps, in an unusual way. – Steve

Cherry Blossoms Echo Spring

Dazzling idea with rainbow and cherry blossoms. – Ted

Fishing Insanity

Delightful. I fish with my husband. It was delightful. Brings back memories. – Sherry

Life in Metamorphosis

That's what we all need. Life is so stressful. It runs full speed all the time. It's hard to let God's peace come in.- Deen

Focus Eyes

Great little Acrostic. You did a great job. Loved reading it. – Gungalo

Chapter Four

Author Bibliography

Some experiences are never forgotten, as in early August, in the summer of 1991. My professional Registered Nurse career suddenly took a parachute nose dive and crashed on the ground, without the safety cord being pulled. All due to an acquired, work related hospital illness that left me permanently disabled. My feelings were mixed. Thinking that we could handle this drastic change in our lives. But how would my retirement deficit, now be funded? Right then I didn't have the slightest clue.

It was hard to leave behind the old familiar employer, co-workers, patients and friends, in the nursing environment on my final departure. The sensation of dread, pain; insecurity, left an uncertainty about the future. However all was not doom or gloom, after leaving the employee parking lot for the last time that cloudy day. With a somber face, I drove home to tell hubby the terrible, sad news.

Roughly eight months later, while lying in bed, my mind drifted in flashback as I recalled part of our wedding vows which said, "In sickness and in health, until death do you part." It was my firm commitment and unbreakable bond in thinking. Later that week an unexpected challenge arose.

After my respiratory treatment, my hubby said, " I am leaving you. It's hard seeing you sick in bed like this." The bedroom door closed with a click. He left me alone. Oh how much darker that day became for me. The tears blinded my eyes as the anxiety wrapped its cold, clammy arms around my sickly body, lying in our bedroom, wondering, why leave me, when I needed you the most?

Shocked! My thoughts were, if only there were a wide mouth megaphone within my reach, the neighborhood would hear my frustration, anger and rejection that would roll off my tongue but it never happened, because not any

Author Bibliography

was around. The urge not to lose control was all I could do not to crash our expensive china plates on the floor, my head dropped in solemn prayer, to my God, Jehovah. A faithful support pillar and endurance provider, who rescued me from screaming, in panic anxiety. He would make a way upon, drawing on his reservoir of strength, at this time.

The next morning my neighbor knocked on the door to visit, sensing there was trouble, seeing my husband drive off with his suitcase in our car. Sharing my ordeal, he offered to pitch in to mow the lawn and do any other chores that needed to be done. He asked nothing in return living by Christian principles. How thankful for such a helping hand, at this time in my life. There was no need for medical intervention to combat elevated blood pressure, or medication to help cope with anxiety or worry about panic.

Each day my friends gathered around as I weathered the dark, storm clouds of life. Hubby left my life in shambles but I was extremely thankful for God's divine shepherding.

Upon refocused introspection, my salary would not be enough for me to live on. So the need for a work-at-home part-time employment search was begun. The only other asset for me was writing. It was my passion, but never thought it would be a means to residual income. Yet, after doing a Google search online helped me create my own website, writing quality articles to help other online website owners, to fill their content needs, at no fee, for over seven years. My question remain, how to make income online?

Truthfully, not knowing put me into the black, deep, debt hole. Do not use this approach for your online business. You will learn later that there is a much better way. After going belly up for that length of time, made me realize that running a failing business is pathetic. My fork in the road had now been reached in futility. Eagerly ready to raise the

Author Bibliography

white flag in surrender, my feet became shod with zeal.

Yet, the tears ran like a swift river from my eyes, while the mucous dripped from both nostrils for ten minutes. This was the turning point, in my life. It was just like Steve Job said, "Success is failure in disguise." Failure is a step-by-step plateau up the ladder, until you make it to the top. Then an exhausted sleep over took me, as anxiety eased away naturally, whereby the body could regain its energy.

Taking advantage by using the free online webinars and teleseminars training programs increased my learning skills in marketing. Suddenly, my life took a ninety degree turn, toward the e-book self-publishing platform, through the Kindle KDP Select program. My Poetry Door Knocker book series, is available for your reading pleasure on Amazon.com. This opportunity, as a self-published author has become my new passion to expand my writing skills.

What seemed an impossible task for me has easily now become a reality. How very fast has modern technology changed the way we read books today from the traditional style. This is simply awesome. The ease to purchase your books on demand, ends the problem with book clutter that leaves more time to enjoy more lifestyle family freedom; fun without being tied down with your business chores.

Technology has allowed me to mobilize my core value strengths, leverage expert mentors and take decisive step action in marketing my products on and offline. My greatest hope is that many small entrepreneurs and businesses will see how my business thrives, in cut back and might also want, to duplicate my financial shelter. It's a timely, cost effective strategy for 2014 and beyond. It's OK. "People helping people do cut ice." Nicely.

Chapter Five

Self-Publishing Critique
        For
Self-Publishing Perspectives

   After reading the article written by Kevin Larimer, Author, Agent, Publisher and Editor in chief of Poets & writers Inc., who had a discussion with Jennifer Ciotta, Self-Published author of I Putin and the No Bull S**t Guide to Self-Publishing, made me smile, because the doors have now been pushed wide open, caused by advanced modern technology, now has allowed hopeful writers, access into the Digital Publishing world. Even in the infancy stage, self-publishing books has warp into sprinting speed; although professional help is needed, the writer and team can work together, dealing with customer demand for self-published book authors. They can now satisfy their reader's desires.
   Just one monthly Google search has revealed the new trend, created by customer selection, for more self-published authors is hot. Readers want to make a change in the way books are read. It is great to know that more of this type are making it inside the door and are welcomed.
   Jennifer sees it as getting even hotter down the road. The customer's appetite for reading books online and for downloads to their iPhone and iPad is a turnstile request that now has arrived. She believes some self-published authors will breakthrough some industry major barriers too. Perhaps the New York Times will start to read a self-published book, once in a while. Or in the future, where we will see more self-published authors being interviewed in the National Poets Registry or on Jon Stewart. If you would like to read this exciting article, you can go to Poets & Writers – Nov/Dec 2013 issue.

Chapter Six

Reference Sources

Readjusting my life in extreme trials remains a challenge. My support pillars took me by the hand and guided me out of the life inner sanctum, muck and mire bog. If it were not for their help, my anxiety level would have reached panic stage. What brightened my outlook was the road in Poetry. The experts that peaked my interest were as follows, to expand my new horizon portal as a thriving poet.

  Fanstory.com is an enjoyable platform, where my poetry and writing skills are assessed daily by their team, Review Committee. Poetry classes, contest and achievement awards can be gain here. The pot is sweetened for cash prizes, if you become a member. Help is as easy as your fingertips from people who are concerned about your growth and success, to become the best poet that you can be. All feedback is provided for everything you post there. It's your progress that will move you step-by-step up the ladder to excellence. The best thing is that it's a healthy way for anti-anxiety control. It helped me and will for you.

  Hamlet by Shakespeare concluded an eventuality that no one can trespass – death. His perspective about death said, "It isn't that death doesn't matter, it matters very much, indeed. But the readiness matters more... Shakespeare dying Hamlet is concerned about the state and his worldly reputation. Such values at the end of tragedies are no longer primary values. "The central theme is spirit of man achieving grandeur."- Edward Huber, Robert Ornstein – Hamlet, Shakespeare, The Signet Classics, Robert Ornstein, Moral Vision of Jacobean Tragedy, pages 258, 262.

Reference Sources

After reading Hamlet's tragedy, what really matters at the end of one's life, is to live simply, build strong faith in God; glorify his Universal Sovereign. Why? At death, you leave the world of the living and your voice, silent.

Yet, does death end it all? Interestingly, in the Bible its Perspective explains in quote, the following view point:
"And I hope toward God, which hope these men also look forward to, that there is going to be a resurrection of both the righteous and the unrighteous."

My conclusion and belief, rest in the resurrection hope for the dead, in the future. – The New World Translation of The Holy Scriptures, 2013, Acts 24:15.

John Milton, a Christian poet whose views with Sampson Agonistes and Short Starter Poems, in the Bible with his expanded views and high ideals, made me reflect upon my own relationship with the Sovereign God for poetry. – Crafts Classics, by, T.E. Barker, University of Illinois vii, viii, ix, New York, Appleton and Century Crofts.

Medical and Surgical Nursing 2nd Edition –Brunner, Emmerson, Ferguson; Suddarth. Pages, 30,31.

Poets & Writers, Self-Publishing Perspectives by Kevin Larimer, Editor and Chief, Poets & Writers Inc. page 69.

If you struggle with anxiety behavior problems that need to be managed, Barry McDonagh who suffered with both anxiety and panic episodes wanted a lasting solution than just a coping technique. This is another alternate solution that you can regain control of your life. For more source information about his program, connect with me by telephone to experience a happier life, today. We know that anxiety is a normal pattern in our lives but it doesn't have to be ultimate ruler…

www.ingramcontent.com/pod-product-compliance
Lightning Source LLC
Chambersburg PA
CBHW041804040426
42448CB00001B/38